69543

K

Kalman, Bobbie

19th century girls and
women

GAYLORD M

HISTORIC

COMMUNITIES

19th Century Girls & Women

Bobbie Kalman

 Crabtree Publishing Company

HISTORIC
COMMUNITIES

Created by Bobbie Kalman

For Marnie Spicer,
a 20th Century woman

Editor-in-Chief
Bobbie Kalman

Research
April Fast

Writing team
Bobbie Kalman
April Fast

Managing editor
Lynda Hale

Editors
Niki Walker
Petrina Gentile
Greg Nickles
Lise Gunby
Virginia Mainprize

Special thanks to
National Gallery of Art, MTRCA, Biltmore Estate,
Deborah Johnson and Sherbrooke Village,
Living History Farms, Professor Carmela Patrias,
and Professor Fred Drake

Computer design
Lynda Hale

Photo research
Hannelore Sotzek

Separations and film
Dot 'n Line Image Inc.

Printer
Worzalla Publishing Company

Crabtree Publishing Company

350 Fifth Avenue	360 York Road, RR 4	73 Lime Walk
Suite 3308	Niagara-on-the-Lake	Headington
New York	Ontario, Canada	Oxford OX3 7AD
N.Y. 10118	L0S 1J0	United Kingdom

Cataloging in Publication Data
Kalman, Bobbie
  19th Century Girls and Women

(Historic communities series)
Includes index.
ISBN 0-86505-434-7 (library bound) ISBN 0-86505-464-9 (pbk.)
This book examines various aspects of the lives of girls and
women during the nineteenth century, including educational and
employment opportunities, clothing, pastimes, and marriage.

1. Women—North America—History—19th century—Juvenile
literature 2. Girls—North America—History—19th century—
Juvenile literature 3. North America—Social life and customs—
19th century—Juvenile literature I. Title. II. Series: Kalman,
Bobbie. Historic communities.

HQ1418.K35 1996   j305.4'0973   LC 96-44506
                                       CIP

Contents

Different roles

During the nineteenth century, which was the hundred years between 1801 and 1900, the lives of girls and women were very different from the lives they lead today. Girls were not valued as highly as boys, and females did not have the same rights as males. They had few choices in education, jobs, or marriage partners.

Future wives and mothers

Parents did not want their daughters to become doctors or business people. They wished only that their daughters find men who would marry and support them. Both poor and wealthy parents had this single goal for their daughters.

Head of the household

Whether she lived on a farm or in the city, a woman was responsible for running the household and looking after the children. Cleaning, cooking, and sewing were all considered "women's work." Girls helped their mothers prepare meals and make bread, butter, candles, and soap. For extra money, some women did laundry for other families. Wealthy women spent their time directing their servants and entertaining the friends of their husband.

A change for women

Near the end of the 1800s, the lives of girls and women changed. More girls attended school. Some women started working in factories. Others became teachers, doctors, and lawyers. Women began to demand the same rights enjoyed by men; they were no longer satisfied with having the limited choices they had in the past.

Most girls learned to sew when they were as young as five. Girls and women sewed clothes and quilts and mended clothing that was torn.

Pioneer women and girls made cloth from scratch. They dyed the wool, spun it into yarn, wove the yarn into cloth, and then sewed clothes for the family.

Pioneer girls and women

The old saying "a woman's work is never done" was certainly true for nineteenth-century pioneer women. Not only did women help their husbands with farm work, but they also washed clothes, fetched water from a river or well, and cooked meals. They spun fleece into yarn, wove or knit the yarn into warm fabric, and sewed clothes for the family. With all these chores, pioneer women had little time for themselves.

Chores for pioneer girls

Girls worked hard alongside their mothers. Older girls cooked, sewed, helped with the laundry, worked in the vegetable garden, and watched the younger children. Younger girls fed the chickens, collected eggs, and made candles.

*The woman in the top picture is working on a **loom**, which was used for weaving yarn into cloth. Clothes, blankets, and rugs were woven. Women also worked in the garden growing vegetables and herbs.*

Making candles

Candles provided light for the pioneer home. Making them was a tiring job. Melted animal fat, or **tallow**, was used as candle wax. Dipping long wicks again and again into the hot fat was a slow, messy job, and fingers often got burned!

Churning butter

Girls also made butter. They collected fresh milk and left it in a cool place for a day or two. When cream rose to the top, they poured it into a butter churn. Sisters took turns pumping the churn stick until clumps of butter floated to the top. The butter was then taken out of the churn, washed, salted, and pressed into molds.

Winter stores

During the long, cold winter months, fresh fruits and vegetables could not be grown or bought. In autumn, mothers and daughters spent days preserving and storing enough food to last until the following summer. They mashed apples into applesauce, made them into apple butter, or cut them into strips and strung them up to dry. They pickled vegetables and dried peas and beans for soup. They dug up potatoes, onions, and carrots from the garden and stored them in the root cellar.

Nothing was wasted

Women and their daughters spent evenings sewing and mending clothes by the light of a candle or fire. They used pieces of fabric from worn-out clothing to mend holes and tears in newer clothes. They saved the tiniest scraps to piece together for a patchwork quilt. With cloth that was too worn to use for quilts, they braided or wove rag rugs.

This girl will have to dip the wicks into hot tallow many more times before the candles are ready.

Most pioneer women had to cook meals over a fire in the kitchen fireplace. In later days, women had stoves for cooking. Making meals took a long time because bread had to be baked and vegetables picked from the garden.

A limited education

*Many girls were educated at home by their mother or a **governess**. Governesses were paid to teach subjects such as reading, writing, basic arithmetic, needlework, music and dancing, languages, and "ladylike manners."*

During the nineteenth century, girls rarely went to college. Many did not even attend high school! People thought that "a woman's place was in the home," so girls were taught mainly the skills they would need as wives and mothers.

The country school

Girls who lived in the country were educated in a one-room schoolhouse. Boys and girls from ages six to twelve were all in the same class. They learned reading, writing, arithmetic, and history. Girls were taught sewing, whereas boys learned woodworking. Children went to school only in the winter. During the rest of the year, they stayed at home to help with the farm work.

City schools

In the city, some girls went to religious schools, which were run by churches. Those with little money attended charity schools or did not go to school at all. Some wealthy parents sent their daughters to private all-girls schools or hired a governess to teach their daughters at home.

Teaching was one of the few jobs women were allowed to have. If a teacher married, she was expected to give up her job to raise a family and care for her husband.

Uncomfortable clothing

For much of the nineteenth century, fashions for girls and women were extremely uncomfortable. Women's bodies were restricted by layers of hot and heavy petticoats, tight corsets, cage crinolines, big bustles, and bulky bathing costumes. Even very young girls were dressed in adult fashions that prevented them from running around and playing games.

*All fashionable women wore a **corset** under their clothes. The corset was stiffened with whalebone and laced tightly at the back to make women look slimmer. Sometimes the laces were pulled so hard that women fainted or broke their ribs. When a corset was laced up, it pushed together the organs in a woman's **torso**, causing her to feel weak and ill.*

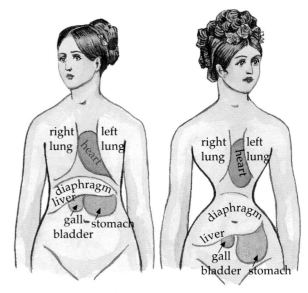

Swimming was a challenge for women because their heavy bathing costumes covered them from the neck to the ankles. The first bathing costumes were made of heavy wool, which was even heavier when it was wet. Some wealthy women hired an assistant to pull them out of the water!

The **cage crinoline** looked like a huge bird cage. It was made of whalebone and cloth and was worn under a skirt. This undergarment made it awkward for women to pass through doorways.

Corsets and crinolines made it very difficult for a woman to bend at the waist. If she dropped something or needed to tie her shoe, a man had to assist her. These undergarments made a woman feel helpless and also kept her from exercising.

Clothing became more comfortable near the end of the nineteenth century. Women wore loose, flowing skirts and **bloomers**, which allowed them to ride bicycles and play sports such as tennis. Exercising made women feel stronger and made them want to be more active in other areas of their lives as well.

Leisure time for women

Wealthy women held tea parties or played cards with their friends. Many became ill because they did very little exercise.

The amount of free time a woman enjoyed usually depended on how much money she had. Some women had many hours of leisure time each week because their servants did the housework. Other women worked all day long. When a woman did have free time, she often called on her friends or neighbors. All women were expected to "pay calls," or make regular visits.

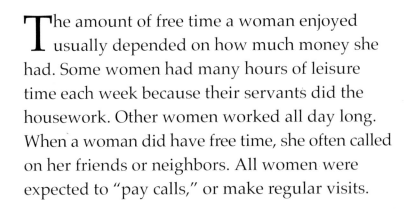

People who had money held huge parties and dances at their homes or at city hotels. To impress others, husbands and fathers spent small fortunes on the dresses of their wives and daughters. Women were treated like expensive showpieces.

City socials

Wealthy women spent their mornings at home, writing letters and assigning household duties to their servants. In the afternoon, they busied themselves with needlework. They often took a stroll in the park or went to a tea party at a friend's home. Some evenings, women dressed in lavish gowns and attended grand balls with their husbands. Couples whirled around the ballroom to the music of an orchestra.

On the farm, women had little leisure time. Work and fun were combined in a bee. At quilting bees, women sewed a large quilt while they talked.

Girls' pastimes

Country girls often had so many chores that they had little time for play. When they did have free time, most girls practiced their needle-work or played with dolls and homemade toys. Skating and tobogganing were favorite winter pastimes. On Sundays, a long sleigh ride also provided fresh air and fun. In summer, some girls liked to spend time in their garden or search the meadows for wildflowers. Swimming and fishing were also popular summer activities.

Little women

Parents encouraged their daughters to play with dolls because they thought it helped prepare girls for motherhood. Many girls enjoyed shopping and hosting tea parties because imitating their mothers made them feel more grown up.

Games

Girls enjoyed skipping and playing hopscotch and string games with their friends. Board games, puzzles, card games, and guessing games were other popular pastimes. Parlor games, such as Blind Man's Buff, were fun to play with a group of friends.

Stitching samplers

Girls practiced their needlework skills by sewing different stitches on a piece of cloth that had letters, verses, and pictures drawn on it. When a girl had covered all the drawings with embroidery, her **sampler** was finished.

This type of embroidery was called a sampler because it showed a sample of a girl's stitching skills.

Three girls' stories

My name is Isabelle. Until last year, I lived in a big city. Then my father decided to move west and start a newspaper in a small village. My life has certainly changed! Instead of attending an all-girls school, I now go to a one-room school. There are boys and girls of different ages in my class.

Instead of taking music lessons, I have lots of chores to do. I milk the cows, churn butter, make candles and soap, and spin wool into yarn. My brothers help my father run the newspaper. They get to have all the fun! When I grow up, I would like to write articles for my father's paper, but he says I'm just a girl and I will be a wife and mother someday. Why can't I write and be a wife and mother, too?

My name is Marika, and I am an immigrant from Hungary. I live on the prairie. To get here, my family and I had to make a long, dangerous journey by boat, wagon, and train. Our home is a sod house, which we built with help from our neighbors. Last week, I started school in a nearby town, and I have to walk two hours each way. I really liked school in Hungary, but I'm having a lot of trouble at this school. I can't understand the teacher because I don't speak much English yet. To make matters worse, the children point at my clothes and giggle. Sometimes I feel very lonely. I miss my friends and grandparents in Hungary, especially "Nagypapa," my grandfather. He taught me how to play the violin. One day, I brought my violin to school and played it during recess. All the kids gathered and listened. They liked my song and clapped. Will they like me, too, someday?

My name is Constance. I am twelve years old, and I am a slave. I live and work on a cotton plantation. My mother used to call me Moesha when we lived together. Moesha is my African name. Mother told me many stories about our family in Africa. She was a house servant for the master at the plantation where I was born. He allowed me to play with his children. They taught me how to read and write, but we had to be carefu the master did not find out. Like most masters, my master was afraid that educated slaves would cause problems. In January of this year, my master died, and I was sold to a very cruel planter. Now I work ten hours a day picking cotton in the hot sun. Sometimes I feel so tired that my bones ache, but I keep on picking so I don't get a whipping. My mother and brothers were sold to different planters. Will I ever see them again?

From girls to women

Girls were considered ready to date, or be **courted**, at the age of sixteen. To look older, they wore long dresses and did their hair in fancy styles. Some parents held **coming-out** parties to present their daughters to society and introduce them to unmarried men. These parties were often formal balls because coming out was considered to be one of the most important events in a girl's life.

The waiting game
A girl never asked a boy to go on a date because it was considered improper and unladylike. A young woman could only hope that the man she liked was also interested in her. If he was, she had to wait until he found the courage to ask her father's permission for them to date.

The watchful eye
Unmarried men and women were not supposed to kiss or even hold hands. In fact, young couples were seldom left alone. Some families paid a **chaperone** to keep an eye on a courting couple. Chaperones were usually older women.

Say it with flowers!
Protective chaperones made it awkward for men and women to court, so couples began sending messages with flowers. Each type of flower had its own meaning. Pansies meant "thinking of you," lilacs meant "first love," and red roses meant "true love." By sending bouquets of a particular flower, a man told a woman how he felt about her without having to say a word.

*Girls who were "coming out" often wore white dresses and were formally introduced to society by their parents. A round of fancy parties followed the girl's **debut**, or introduction, as a young woman.*

Hoping to marry

In the nineteenth century, few women remained unmarried. A girl who was not married by the age of 25 was considered an "old maid." Most girls hoped they would marry because life was difficult for single women. There were few ways for them to earn a living.

Most unmarried women lived with their married sisters. In pioneer times, single women often had the task of spinning fleece into yarn for the family to use. People who did this job were known as "spinsters." Eventually, all unmarried women came to be known as spinsters.

What's love got to do with it?

Couples often married for reasons other than love. Most women needed a man to provide them with a house, clothes, and money. Many men married so that they had someone to look after their home and have their children. Husbands and wives often grew to love one another after they were married.

*Some parents filled a **hope chest** in the hope that their daughter would get married. A hope chest contained items a new bride would need for her home, such as blankets and tablecloths.*

The proposal

A man was expected to get down on one knee when he proposed marriage. If the couple was under the watch of a chaperone, the proposal was written in a letter. Before a man proposed marriage to a woman, he first asked her father's permission.

Wedding vows

The couple usually exchanged wedding vows in a church. The bride's vows included the promise to obey her husband, but his did not include a promise to obey her.

White wedding gowns did not become popular until late in the nineteenth century. Before that time, most brides wore their best dress, regardless of its color.

Childbirth

Some women had to work hard from morning to night. They did not know that they had to rest when they were pregnant.

(above) Some mothers bundled their babies tightly against a board. They thought it made the baby feel secure. Later, people learned that it was healthier for a baby to move his or her arms and legs freely. (opposite page) As people learned more about how to stay healthy, fewer women and babies died.

In the early 1800s, giving birth was dangerous for both a mother and her baby. People knew little about germs or proper nutrition. In some areas, there were no doctors or **midwives** to help pregnant women. A midwife is a woman who assists with childbirth.

Lack of good food and rest

Most nineteenth-century families were large. It was common for a woman to be pregnant more than ten times! Many pregnant women became ill because they did not eat enough nutritious foods to keep themselves healthy. Some became exhausted because they did not have help with their many chores. Babies sometimes died before they were born because their mothers were tired or sick. All too often, mothers and babies died during childbirth.

Danger of infections

The medical instruments doctors sometimes used during difficult births were not **sterilized**, or cleaned of germs. As a result of these dirty instruments, many women and babies suffered from infections.

Changes for mothers and babies

By the end of the century, pregnant women knew more about how to care for themselves than women did in the early 1800s. They had healthier diets, and they found time to rest during their pregnancies. Sterilized tools and new medicines also meant fewer infections after childbirth. As a result of these changes, more mothers and babies survived.

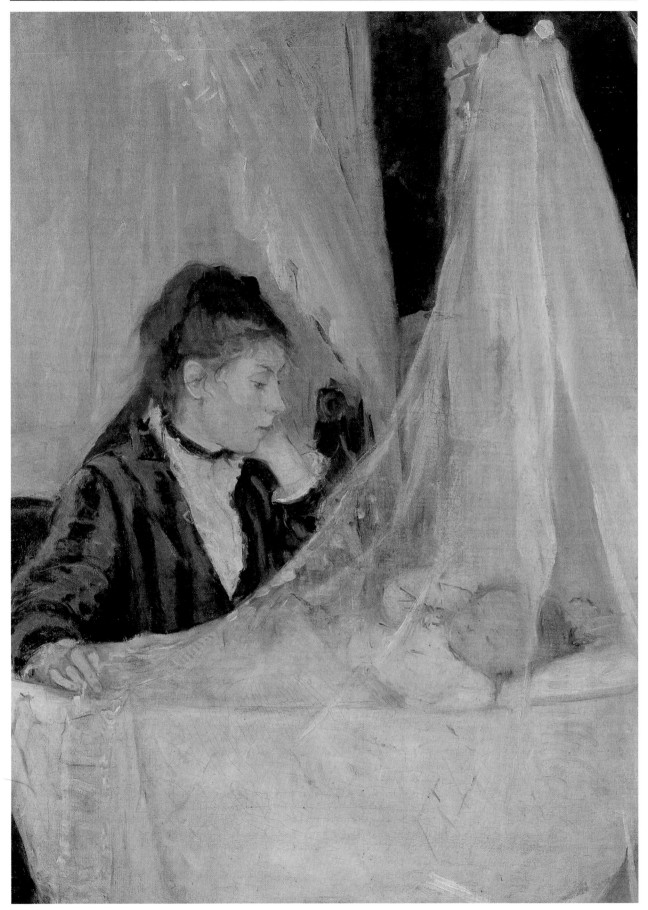

Jobs for women

There were few paying jobs available to women. Some earned extra money by bringing work into their home. Others worked as servants, nurses, teachers, or factory laborers.

Washing and sewing

Doing other people's laundry was one way to earn extra money. Washing clothes was hard work because laundry had to be scrubbed on a washboard and wrung out by hand. Taking in extra laundry was tiring for women who already had enough housework to keep them busy.

Women also sewed and mended other people's worn clothing. If a woman was talented at sewing clothes, she was called a **seamstress**. A seamstress could earn a good living by making fancy new clothes for other people.

Teaching

Some women taught school, and others worked as governesses. Women were paid less than men for teaching and were allowed to teach only until they were married.

Labor in the factories

The **Industrial Revolution** changed the lives of many women. During this period, factories and machines were introduced to make products quickly. Women flocked to cities to find work in the new factories. Factory owners hired women because they could pay them less than they paid men for the same job. Women were willing to work long hours under terrible conditions because few other jobs were available to them.

Many women left their parents' farms to move to the city. They worked long hours for low pay in factories.

Women were not allowed to attend medical school until the late 1800s, so nurses were trained on the job.

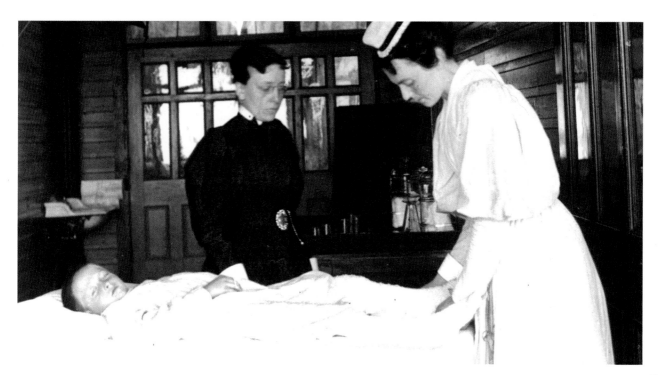

Women who had servants had a lot of free time. Often, they felt bored, sad, and lonely because they had nothing to do and no one to talk to. Even their husbands did not discuss much with them.

Big changes needed

Many women were bored because they did not work and had too much free time. Doing **charitable work** was one way to fill their day. Charitable work is unpaid work that helps people who are less fortunate. Helping people in hospitals and soup kitchens showed women that they had useful skills. Working outside the home also showed them that they were neither weak nor helpless, as many people had believed. These discoveries gave women confidence.

Women in need of help

Volunteers found that those who needed help were usually women and orphaned children. They learned that many women had very difficult lives.

Few rights

In the 1800s, women had few rights. The laws treated them as if they were their husband's property. Women were not allowed to vote, and once they were married, everything they owned became the property of their husband. If a couple divorced, the husband kept the children and all the money, property, and possessions. Big changes were needed to improve the lives of all women!

"We want equal rights!"

Women wanted the chance to attend the schools and colleges that were open only to male students. They wanted to be paid the same amount as men for doing the same work. They demanded better jobs, the opportunity to have careers, and the right to vote. Women began a struggle for equal rights called the **women's movement**.

Women gained self-confidence by working as volunteers in hospitals and soup kitchens.

In the 1800s, women could vote only in some local elections. Members of the women's movement believed that women should vote in federal elections, too. Although many people fought hard to stop them, Canadian women finally gained this right in 1918, followed by those in the United States in 1920.

Making a difference

Many nineteenth-century women were pioneers in the world of education, work, and the women's movement. They stood up for what they believed was right, even though a lot of people disagreed with them. Here are just a few of their stories.

Elizabeth Cady Stanton

Susan B. Anthony

Susan B. Anthony and Elizabeth Cady Stanton were American women who worked together for the women's movement. They spoke in public about women's rights and encouraged other women to join the fight. In 1868 they started *Revolution*, the first newspaper run by women. They wrote stories about women's rights to make people aware of the women's movement and to inspire other women to join their cause.

Elizabeth Blackwell was the first woman to work as a doctor in the United States. When she first applied to medical schools, she was rejected. One medical college finally agreed to let her in, but only if every male student voted to accept her. The students did not take the request seriously. As a joke, they all voted to let her in! When she graduated in 1849, the college made a rule that no more women would be admitted. Elizabeth created a new school called the Women's Medical College of the New York Infirmary for Women and Children. Other women's colleges opened shortly after.

Elizabeth Blackwell

Emily Stowe was one of six daughters born to a family in Ontario, Canada. She studied hard to be a teacher and soon became the first female principal in Canada. Emily then decided to study medicine, but no medical school in Canada would accept her because she was a woman. In the United States, however, attitudes were slowly changing, thanks to a few courageous women. Emily attended a medical school in New York and, in 1867, became the first female doctor to practice in Canada. For most of her life, she worked for women's rights. She was the first president of the Dominion Women's Enfranchisement Association, an organization that helped Canadian women gain the right to vote.

Emily Stowe

Susan La Flesche

Susan La Flesche, the daughter of an Omaha Chief, was born on a reservation in Nebraska. She was the first Native American woman to become a doctor. She studied medicine at the Women's Medical College of Pennsylvania in Philadelphia and was such an excellent student that she finished her studies in only three years. After becoming a doctor, she returned to the Omaha reservation and traveled great distances to visit her many patients. Besides being a doctor, Susan acted as a translator and financial adviser. She raised money to build a hospital on the reservation so her patients could come to her.

Mary Ann Shadd

Mary Ann Shadd was born a **free black** in Delaware. Free blacks were African Americans who, during the time of slavery, were not slaves. In 1850, a law called the **Fugitive Slave Act** was passed. Under this law, both runaway slaves and free blacks could be captured and sent into slavery. To protect her freedom, Mary fled to Ontario, Canada. She began a school for African Americans who went to Canada from the United States. She started a newspaper, making her the first African American female publisher in North America. She also became the first African American woman to complete her law degree in the United States. With her legal expertise, Mary approached the Judiciary Committee of the United States House of Representatives and argued for the right of women to vote. She won her case and was one of the first women to vote in a federal election in the United States.

Harriet Tubman fought for the equality of African Americans as well as women. She was born a slave on a Maryland plantation. Her desire for freedom led her to escape on the **Underground Railroad**. The Underground Railroad was a network of people who provided transportation and safe shelter for people escaping slavery. Harriet went north to Pennsylvania, where slavery was illegal. She then risked her life by returning south to guide other slaves north. After the Fugitive Slave Act was passed, Harriet helped many slaves escape to freedom in Canada. When slavery was finally abolished, Harriet took up the fight for women's rights.

Harriet Tubman

Glossary

abolish To put an end to something

bee A gathering of people that combines work with fun

bloomers Women's loose, baggy trousers that end at the knee

bustle A pad or hoop that adds fullness to the back of a skirt

chaperone A person, usually an older, married woman, paid to supervise a young, unmarried couple

charitable work Volunteer work to help people who are less fortunate

coming-out party A formal ball to introduce young women to society and especially to unmarried men

corset A stiff undergarment that was laced tightly on a woman's upper body; also called a stay

debut The formal introduction of a young woman to society

embroidery Decorative stitching done with colored thread

governess A woman paid to teach and train children in their home

hope chest A chest used by a young woman to collect fine linens and household items in preparation for her marriage

immigrant A person who moves to another country to make a new home

Industrial Revolution In North America, the period beginning in the mid-19th century when people began using steam-powered and electrical machines to make products

loom A large machine that weaves thread or yarn into cloth

master The owner of a slave

midwife A woman who assists women in childbirth

needlework Work, such as sewing, knitting, or embroidery, that is done with a needle

petticoat A long skirt worn underneath a dress or skirt

pioneer A person who settles in a new territory; also a person who is first to open a new area of thought, research, or activity

plantation A large farm where one type of crop, such as cotton or tobacco, is grown

planter The owner of a plantation

reservation Land that is set aside by the government for use by the First Nations

root cellar A cool place built under a house or into a hillside and used to store fruits and vegetables

sampler A decorative piece of cloth embroidered with designs or letters

seamstress A woman skilled in sewing

showpiece Something put on display

slave A person who is considered to be the property of another person

soup kitchen A place where free food is given to people who cannot afford to buy their own

sterilize To remove dirt and bacteria

tallow Melted animal fat that is used to make candles and soap

torso The trunk of the body, not including the head or limbs

Underground Railroad A secret network of people who helped runaway slaves reach areas in which there was no slavery

whalebone A strong, thin material from the jaws of baleen whales that was used to stiffen a corset or crinoline

women's movement The actions of women who have fought for equal rights, such as the right to vote

Index

Acknowledgments

Photographs and reproductions
Courtesy of Biltmore Estate, Asheville, NC: title page
Bridgeman/Art Resource, NY: cover, pages 4, 21
Giraudon/Art Resource, NY: pages 8, 24
Bobbie Kalman: page 6 (top)
Erich Lessing/Art Resource, NY: pages 13, 23
Living History Farms: page 5 (top)
Diane Payton Majumdar: page 3
MTRCA: pages 5 (bottom), 6 (bottom), 7 (both), 13

National Museum of American Art, Washington DC/Art Resource, NY: page 16
Reuters/Archive Photos: page 18
David Schimpky: page 15
Tate Gallery, London/Art Resource, NY: pages 12, 14 , 26

Illustrations and colorizations
Barbara Bedell: cover, title page, pages 9 (both), 10-11, 14 , 15, 17 (both), 20, 22 (both), 25 (top), 27 (both), 28-30 (all)
Lynda Hale: pages 24, 25 (bottom)
Janet Kimantas: page 19

1 2 3 4 5 6 7 8 9 0   Printed in the U.S.A.   6 5 4 3 2 1 0 9 8 7